This book belongs to:

_____

Text and Illustrations copyright © 2011 by Characters of Character
Printed By:
Characters of Character NFP, Inc.
P.O. Box 391
McHenry, Illinois 60050

Follow us on twitter at cofcjoni
Like us on facebook https://www.facebook.comCharactersOfCharacterNonprofit/
Follow us on Pinterest at https://www.pinterest.com/jonidowney/
Connect on LinkedIn with Joni Downey

All rights reserved. No part of this publication may be reproduced or transmitted in any form or by any means, electronic, photocopying, recording, or otherwise, without the prior written permission of Characters of Character NFP, Inc.

Printed in the United States of America

Cool Characters

Behavior Bear

Do'er Duck

Friendship Frog

Healthy Hippo

Manners Monkey

Respectful Rabbit

Responsible Rabbit

Self-Esteem Elephant

Warm-Hearted Walrus

Having character is cool!

I am Warm-Hearted Walrus. I am kind. I love when others show kindness. I am always a buddy, and never a bully.

Draw the other half of my body below using the grid as a guide.

I am Self-Esteem Elephant. I take pride in everything that I do. I love when other people feel as confident as I do.

Solve each problem. Color the answers less than 20 gray and the answers greater than 20 tan.

I am Responsible Rabbit. I take responsibility for my own actions. I am also responsible for my belongings, so I am always sure to put my things away after I am done playing with them. Draw me a picture of your favorite belonging. Then, on the lines below write down how you take responsibility for your belongings.

_____
_____
_____
_____

I am proud of you for being so responsible!

I am Healthy Hippo. Each day I make sure that I take care of my body and mind. I love fruits and vegetables! Connect the dots to find out what else I love to do.

I am Respectful Rabbit. I show respect to my teacher by sitting quietly in my seat and listening to what she has to say. I show respect to my pets by making sure that I always play nicely with them. I show respect to my toys by putting them away after I am done playing with them. Can you come up with different words out of the phrase below? Write down what you find in the box below. I've already found one word for you!

I AM RESPECTFUL

Cat

I am Friendship Frog. I am always honest and nice to my friends. I like to play games with my friends. Do you? Find a friend to play tic-tac-toe with in the boxes below.

www.charactersofcharacter.org

I am Do'er Duck. I never give up on a task, no matter how difficult it may be. I persevere. Do you know what persevering means? It means to never give up. Sometimes I need to ask for help to finish my tasks. Could you help me unscramble the following phrases? If you need help, there's a word bank on my flowerpot below.

1. EVEELIB _____

2. RSEEREVPE _____

3. RNEEV VIEG PU _____

4. YSWALA YRT _____

5. I DDI TI _____

6. PEKE NGYRTI _____

7. VIEHCEA _____

8. OD UOYR STBE _____

9. VIETISPO TTTDUEAI _____

Persevere	Never give up	Do your best
Always try	Keep trying	Achieve
I did it	Positive attitude	Believe

Answer Key: 1) Believe 2) Persevere 3) Never give up 4) Always try 5) I did it 6) Keep trying 7) Achieve 8) Do your best 9) Positive attitude

I am Behavior Bear. I behave at home when I do what my parents ask of me without being told twice. How do you behave at home? Draw a picture of you using good behavior at home in the box below. You should be proud of yourself for having good behavior!

GOOD BEHAVIOR

SHOW RESPECT

FRIENDLY

BE PROUD

CHARACTER

PERSEVERE

BE RESPONSIBLE

GOOD MANNERS

BE KIND

BE HEALTHY

Your name
Your address
Your city and zip code

Put stamp here

Characters of Character
Name of Character
P.O. Box 391
McHenry, Illinois 60050

The Characters of Character would love to hear from you at any time! We enjoy getting mail from boys and girls and we always write back to you. Please include a Self-Addressed Stamped Envelope so we can reply to your letter. Remember to ask an adult if you need help with this. We can't wait to meet you!

Made in the USA
Monee, IL
07 February 2024